1000 SIGHT WORDS
THE ULTIMATE VOCABULARY BOOK

PICTURE DICTIONARY WITH SENTENCE

English - Turkish

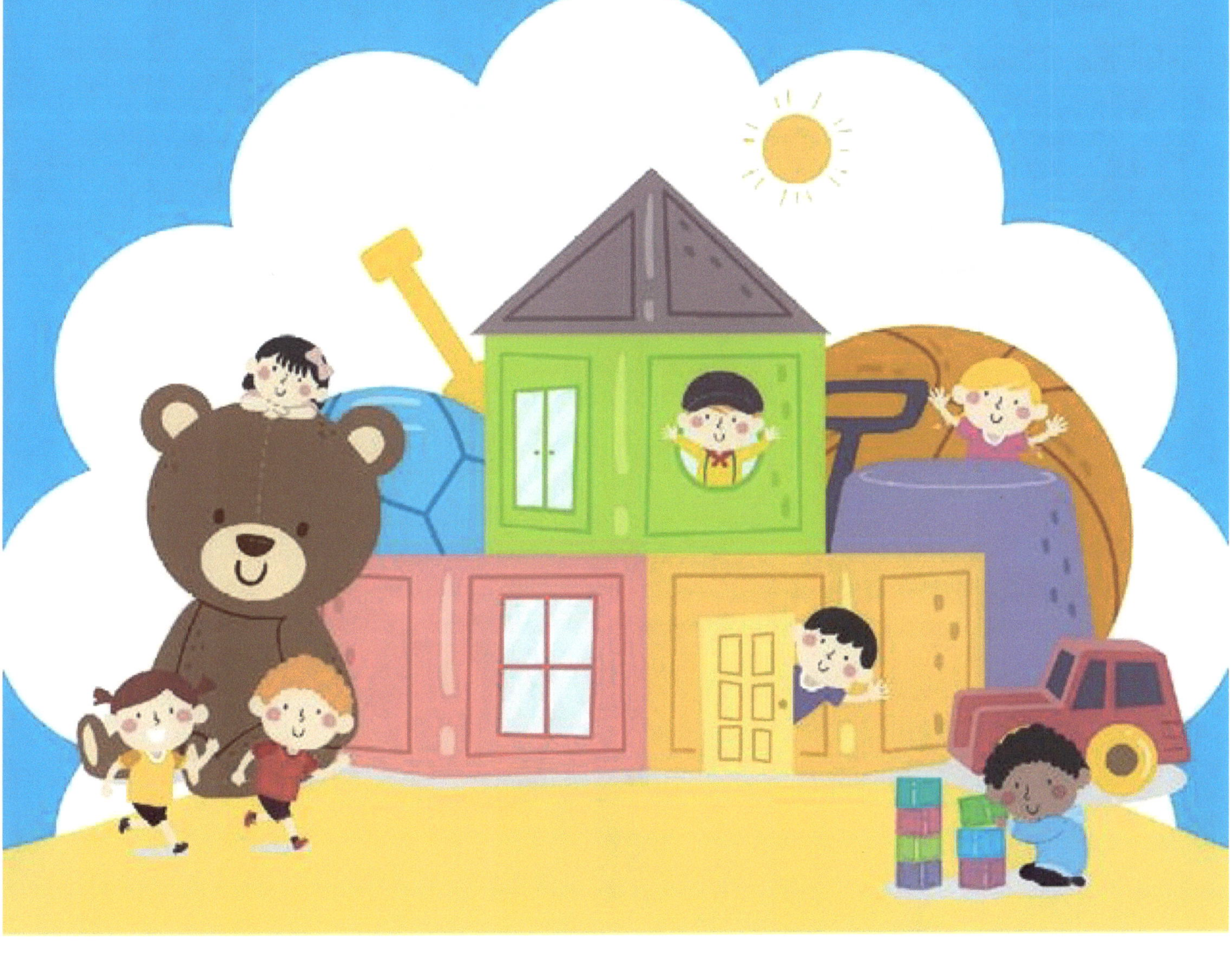

action

hareketler

Action!

actually

aslında

I actually like strawberry.

adjective

sıfat

Tell me an adjective to describe this.

afraid

korkmuş

What are you afraid of?

agreed

katılıyorum

They agreed on music.

ahead

önde

Who was ahead in the race?

allow

izin vermek

Did the teacher allow him to go play?

apple

elma

Eat an apple.

arrived

geldi

My plane arrived on time.

born

doğan

Where were you born?

bought

satın almak

She bought new clothes.

British

ingiliz

Who is the British monarch?

capital

başkent

The capital is in Washington DC.

chance

şans

Dice is a game of chance.

chart

grafik

What does your medical chart say?

church

kilise

Did you go to church?

column

kolon

Did you read the newspaper column?

company

şirket

What company do you work for?

conditions

koşullar

What are the weather conditions.

corn

mısır

Do you like corn?

cotton

pamuk

A q-tip is made of cotton.

cows

inek

How many cows does he have?

create

oluşturmak

What art did you create?

dead

ölü

The bug is dead.

deal

anlaştık mı

Did you agree on the deal?

death

ölüm

The grim reaper is death.

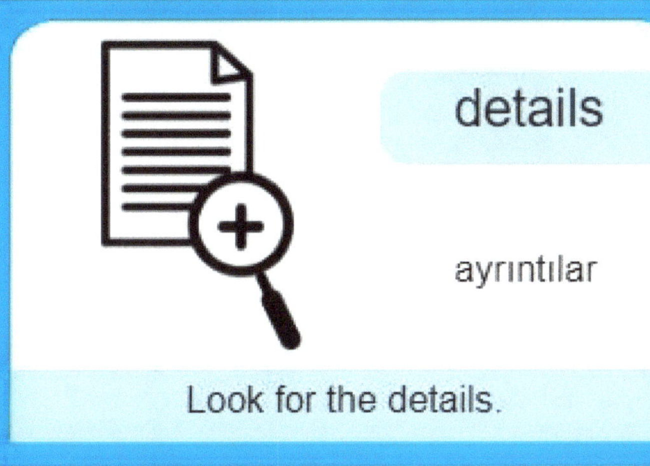

details

ayrıntılar

Look for the details.

determine

belirlemek

Did you determine where to go eat?

difficult

zor

I found this difficult.

division

bölünme

We did division today.

doesn't

değil

Doesn't it sound beautiful?

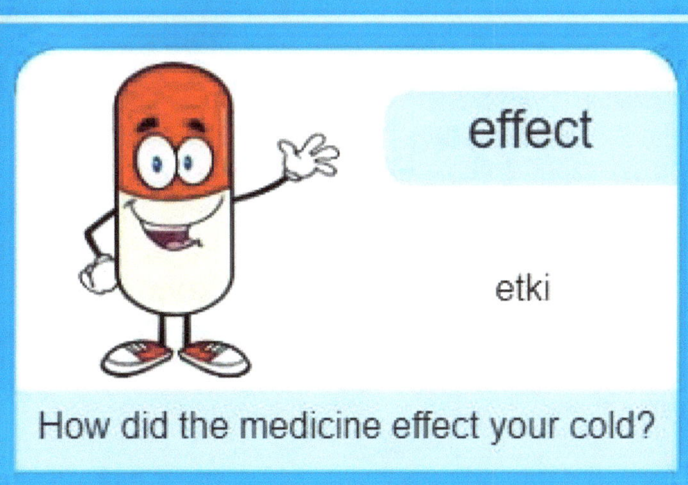

effect

etki

How did the medicine effect your cold?

entire

tüm

The entire family was in the picture.

especially

özel

She especially liked writing.

evening

akşam

The ceremony was this evening.

experience

deneyim

She has a lot of experience.

factories

fabrikalar

There are a lot of factories there.

fair

eğlence parkı

Let's go to the fair.

fear

korku

I have a huge fear of clowns.

fig

incir

I ate a fig.

forward

ileri

Spring forward the clocks.

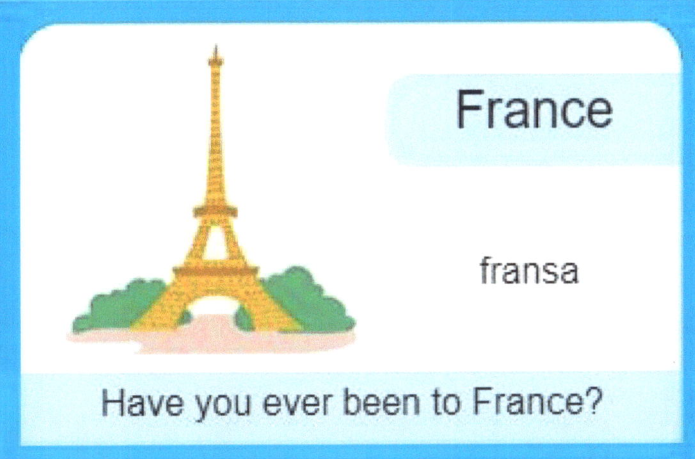

France

fransa

Have you ever been to France?

fresh

taze

All the fruit is fresh.

Greek

yunan

Have you ever had Greek food?

gun

silahlar

We played with a water gun.

hoe

çapa

Use a hoe in the garden.

huge

kocaman

Those trees are huge!

isn't

değil

Isn't it nice to hang out with friends?

led

önder

The dog led her.

level

seviye

Use the level to hang the picture.

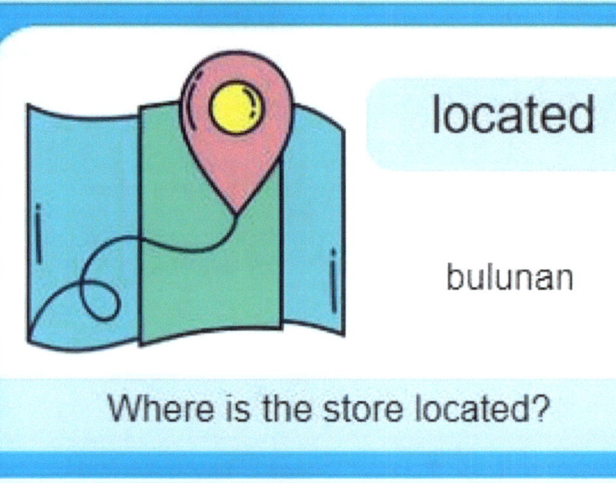

located

bulunan

Where is the store located?

march

geçit

Are you going to march with the band?

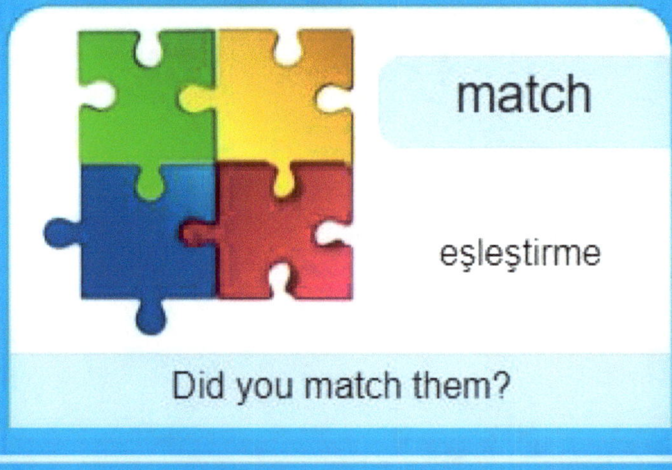

match

eşleştirme

Did you match them?

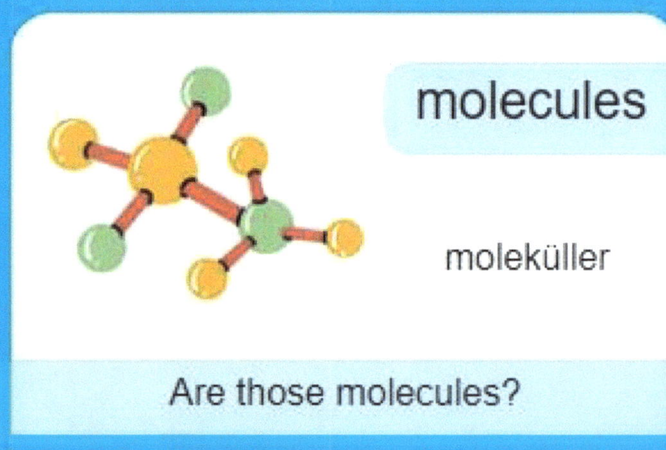

molecules

moleküller

Are those molecules?

northern

kuzeyinde

He lives in northern California.

nose

burun

My nose is running.

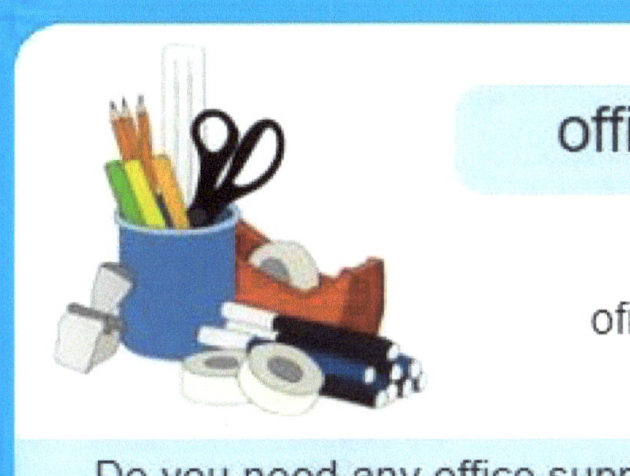

office
ofis

Do you need any office supplies?

oxygen
oksijen

What is the symbol for oxygen?

plural
çoğul

What is the plural of a mouse?

prepared
hazırlamak

She prepared for the exam.

pretty
güzel

Pretty in pink.

printed
basılı

She printed out the forms.

radio
radyo

Let's listen to the radio.

repeated
tekrar et

They repeated the exercises daily.

rope

ip

Do you have any rope?

rose

gül

Thank you for the rose.

score

puan

What was the final score?

seat

oturma yeri

The girls took a seat in the sand.

settled

yerleşik

The case was settled.

shoes

ayakkabı

Put your shoes on.

shop

dükkanlar

I'm need to go shop for groceries.

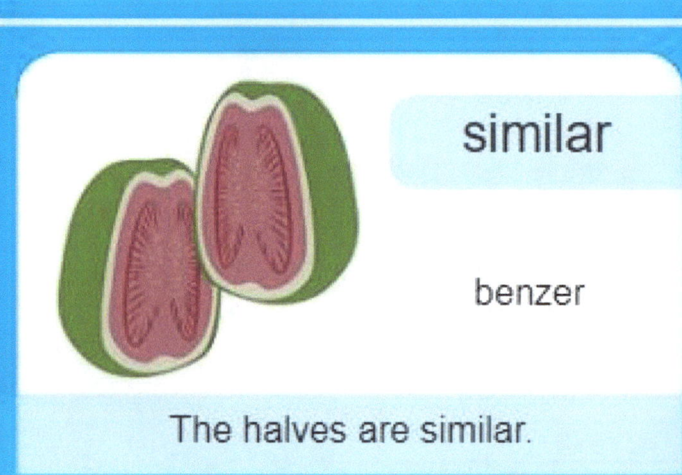

similar

benzer

The halves are similar.

sir

bayım

Yes, sir!

sister

kız kardeş

Is she your sister?

smell

koku

I love the smell of cookies!

solution

çözüm

I figured out a solution!

southern

güney

She's a southern belle.

steel

çelik

The new building used steel.

stretched

gergin

We stretched before the workout.

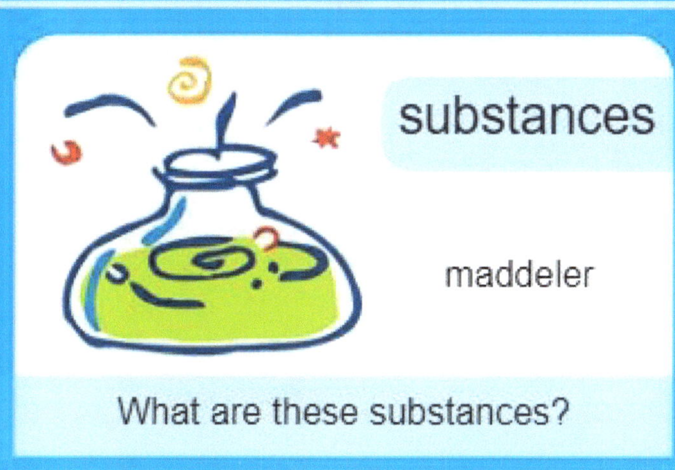

substances

maddeler

What are these substances?

suffix

sonek

What is the suffix of the word?

sugar

şeker

Sugar cube for your tea?

tools

araçlar

May I borrow your tools?

total

toplam

What's the total?

track

izlemek

The runners got on the track.

triangle

üçgen

How many sides does a triangle have?

truck

kamyon

Is thaty our truck?

underline

<u>underline</u>

altını çizmek

Underline the word.

various

çeşitli

I watch various shows.

view

görünüm

That is a beautiful view!

Washington

washington

She is from Washington.

we'll

niyet

We'll finish buying our groceries.

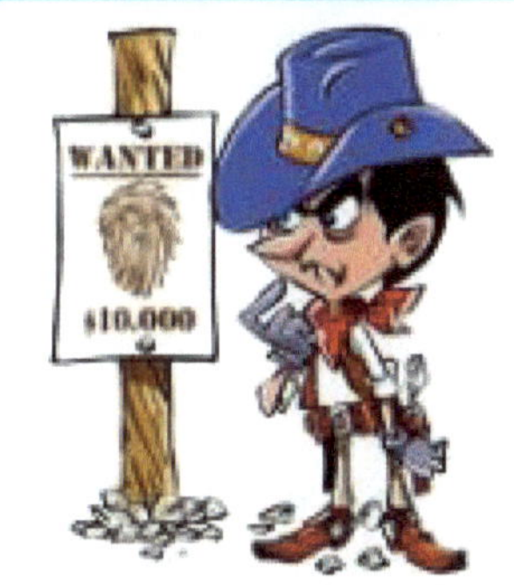

western

batı

It's western wear day.

win

kazanmak

Did you win?

woman

kadın

The woman was on her way to work.

workers

çalışan

The workers were busy.

wouldn't

değil

Wouldn't you like to go shopping?

wrong

yanlış

Did I get it wrong?

yellow

sarı

A banana is yellow.

after

sonra

You may have dessert after dinner.

again

tekrar

May we go on the ride again?

air

hava

The air was cold.

also

ayrıca

I also like baseball.

America

amerika

Columbus sailed to America.

animal

hayvan

My favorite animal is a lion.

another

bir diğeri

Have another cookie.

answer

cevap

Raise your hand to answer.

any

hiç

Do you have any crayons?

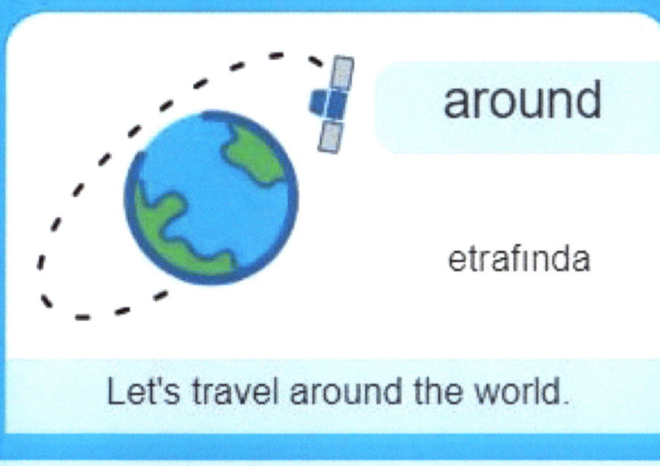

around

etrafında

Let's travel around the world.

ask

sor

It's good to ask questions.

away

uzakta

Throw your trash away.

back

geri

We went back to school.

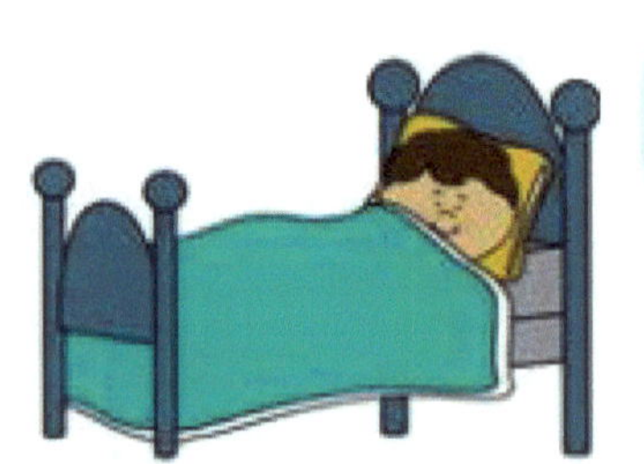

because

çünkü

I went to bed because I was tired.

before

önce

Sharpen your pencil before the test.

big

büyük

The elephant is a big animal.

boy

oğlan

The boy played a basketball.

came

geldi

He came to class.

change

değişiklik

I save my change.

different

farklı

They use different balls.

does

yapmak

Does he ride the bus?

end

son

She watched to the end.

even

hatta

They learned about even numbers.

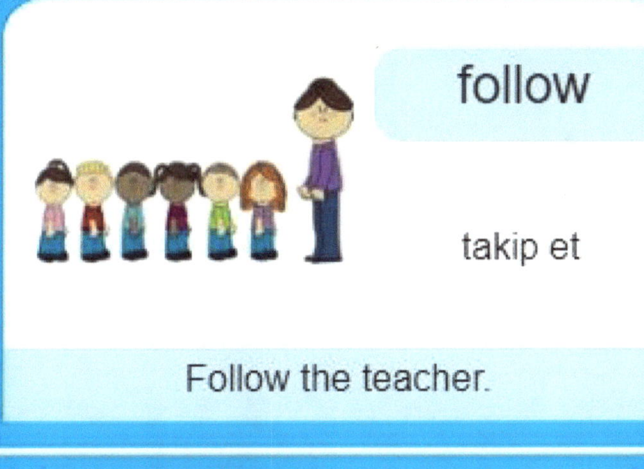

follow

takip et

Follow the teacher.

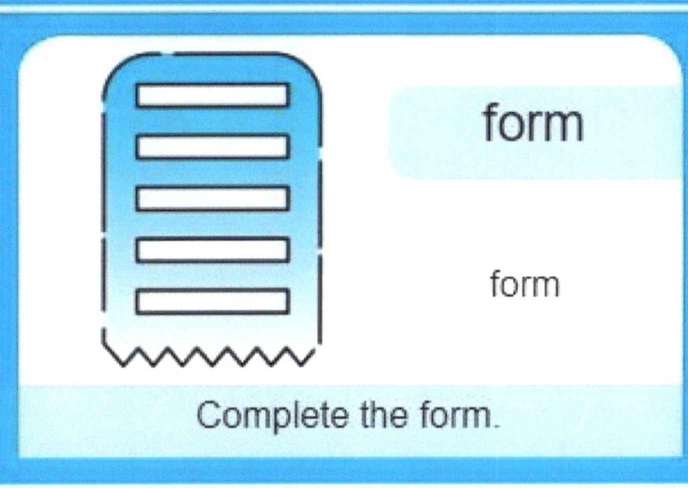

form

form

Complete the form.

found

bulundu

We found a puppy.

give

vermek

I like to give gifts.

good

iyi

The hamburger was good.

great

harika

Great job!

hand
el
Please hand in your work.

help
yardım
You should help others.

here
buraya
Do you sit here?

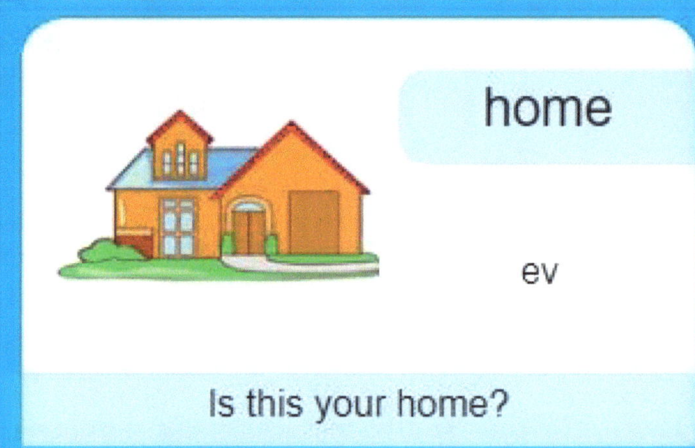

home
ev
Is this your home?

house
ev
The doll house was pink.

just
sadece
The train just left.

kind
nazik ol
Be kind to each other.

know
bilmek
I don't know.

land

arazi

They bought some land.

large

büyük

A bear is large.

learn

öğrenmek

It's fun to learn science.

letter

mektup

He mailed a letter.

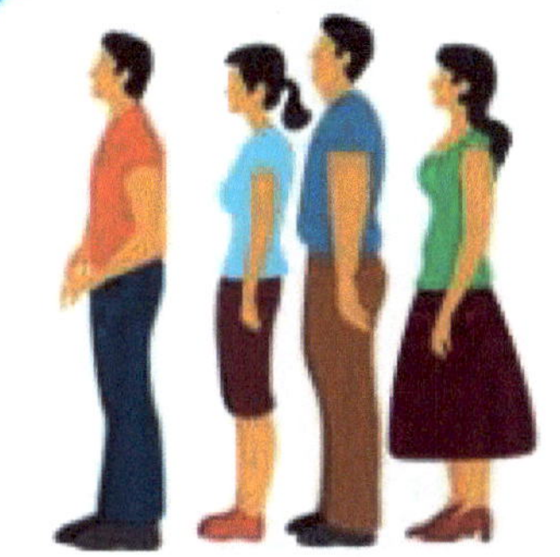

line

hatlar

Please form a line.

little

küçük

He has a little sister.

live

canlı

You live in the city.

man

adam

The man drove.

me

ben mi

Come with me to the park.

means

anlamına geliyor

She got her by means of a taxi.

men

erkekler

The men played football.

most

çoğu

Most students like to help.

mother

anne

He loves his mother.

move

hareket

His family decided to move.

much

çok

How much is the camera?

must

zorunlu

You must raise your hand.

name

isim

What is his name?

need

istemek

Do you need to sleep?

new

yeni

We have a new teacher.

off

kapalı

The rocket blasted off.

old

eski

Those are old toys.

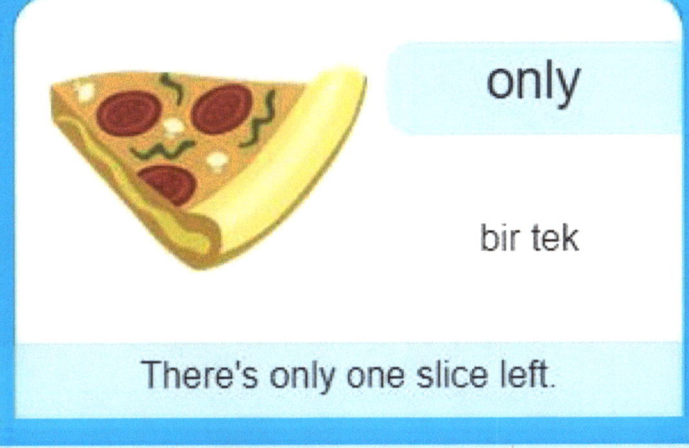

only

bir tek

There's only one slice left.

our

bizim

She was our teacher.

over

bitmiş

He jumped over it.

page

sayfa

Please turn the page.

picture

resim

They took their picture.

place

yerler

This is my favorite place.

play

oyna

Let's play together!

point

nokta

Point the way.

put

koymak

Please put the supplies away.

read

okumak

Do you like to read?

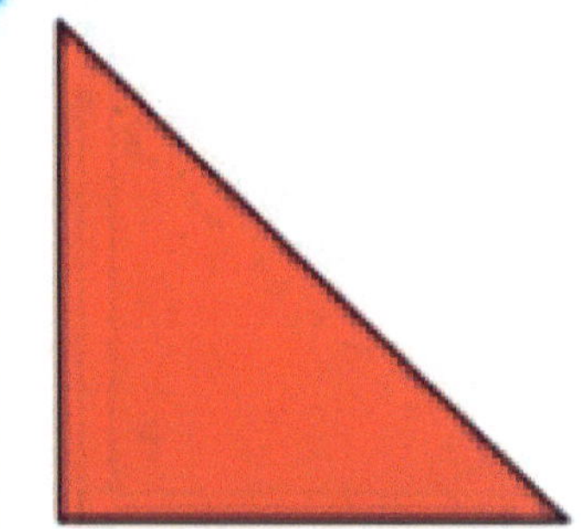

right

sağ

That's a right triangle.

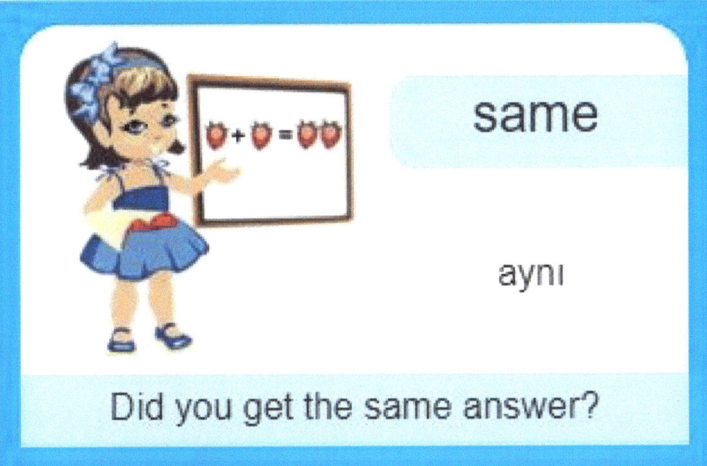

same

aynı

Did you get the same answer?

say

söyle

What did you say?

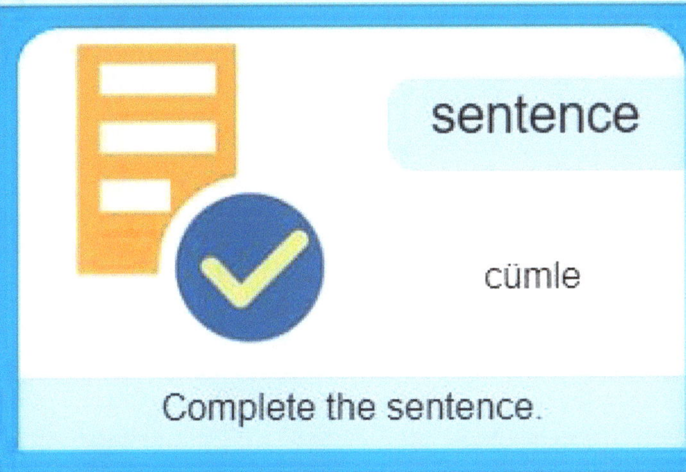

sentence

cümle

Complete the sentence.

set

ayarlamak

Please set the table.

should

meli

We should exercise.

show

göstermek

Show your work.

small

küçük

The ladybug is small.

sound

ses

A bee makes a buzzing sound.

spell

harf harf kodlamak

Please spell the word.

still

yine

I still want ice skates.

study

ders çalışma

It's time to study.

such

böyle

He is such a good dog.

take

almak

Please take your seat.

tell

söylemek

She wanted to tell a secret.

things

bir şeyler

She washed a lot of things.

think

düşünmek

Think about it.

three

üç

It's the number three.

through

vasıtasıyla

He was through with the race.

too

çok

Do you like chocolate too?

try

deneyin

Try again, please.

turn

çevirmek

Turn in your homework.

us

bize

She taught us.

very

çok

He is a very good singer.

want

istemek

I want to ride my bike.

well

iyi

You did well.

went

gitti

We went to recess.

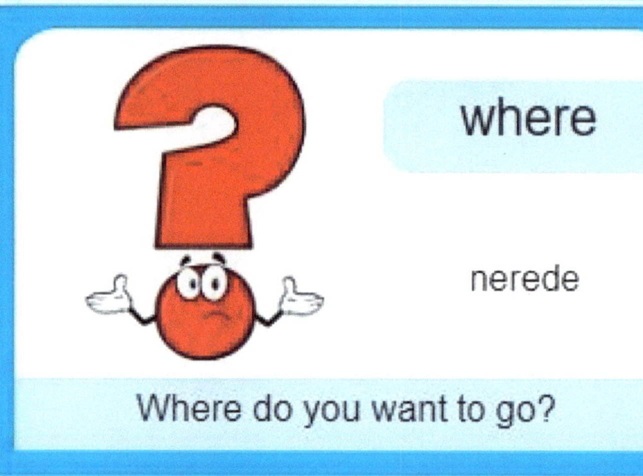

where

nerede

Where do you want to go?

why

neden

She asked why?

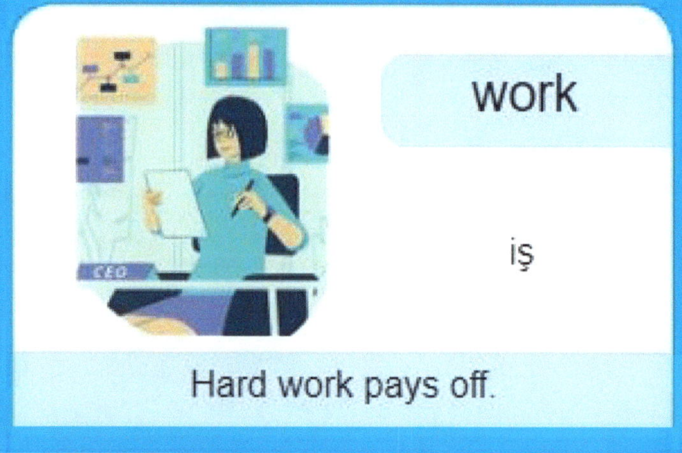

work

iş

Hard work pays off.

world

dünya

I want to travel the world.

years

yıl

You are five years old today.

above

yukarıda

The sky was above them.

add

ekle

If you add one plus two, you get three.

almost

neredeyse

It's almost lunch time.

along

boyunca

We get along.

always

her zaman

She always brushes her teeth.

began

başladı

The baby began to cry.

begin

başla

You may begin your exam.

being

olmak

She is being shy.

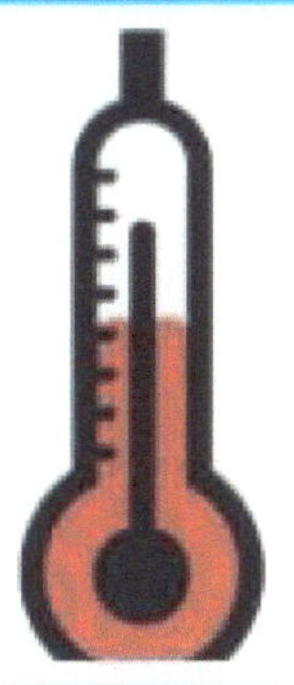

below

altında

It's below thirty degrees.

between 123 arasında Two is between one and three.	 **book** kitap I'm reading this book.
 **both** her ikisi de They both worked on math.	 **car** araba He bought a new car.
 **carry** taşımak She had a bag to carry her groceries.	 **children** çocuklar Four children sang.
 **city** kent He worked in the city.	 **close** kapat Please close the door.

country

ülke

Do you live in the country?

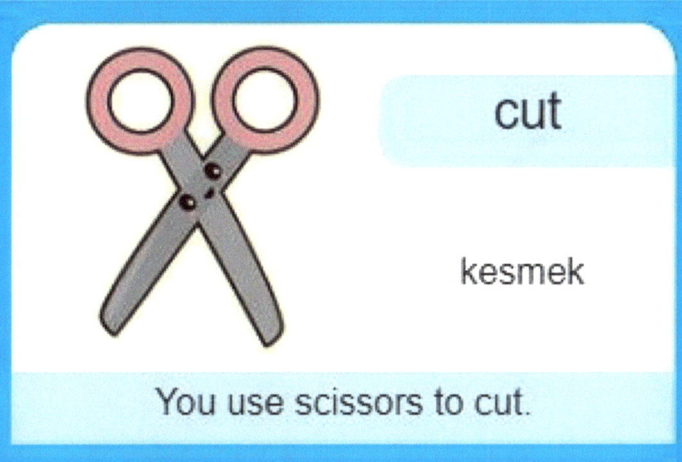

cut

kesmek

You use scissors to cut.

don't

değil

Don't forget!

earth

dünya

Our planet is Earth.

eat

yemek

I eat bananas.

enough

yeter

Did you eat enough pancakes?

every

her

I shower every day.

example

misal

This is an example of a bird.

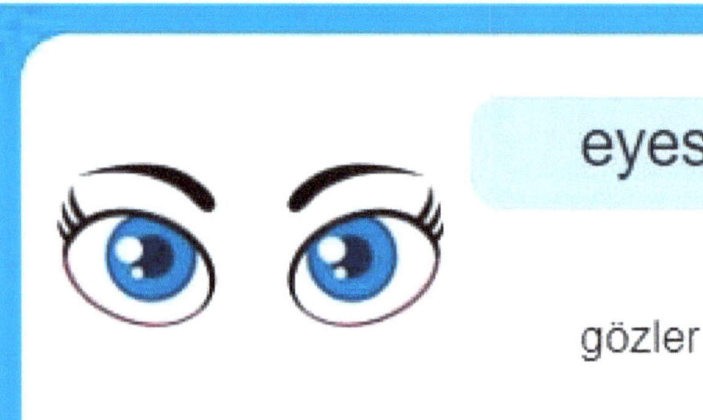

eyes

gözler

What color are her eyes?

face

yüz

They were at the face painting booth.

family

aile

How big is your family?

far

irak

How far is it?

father

baba

Her father walked her to school.

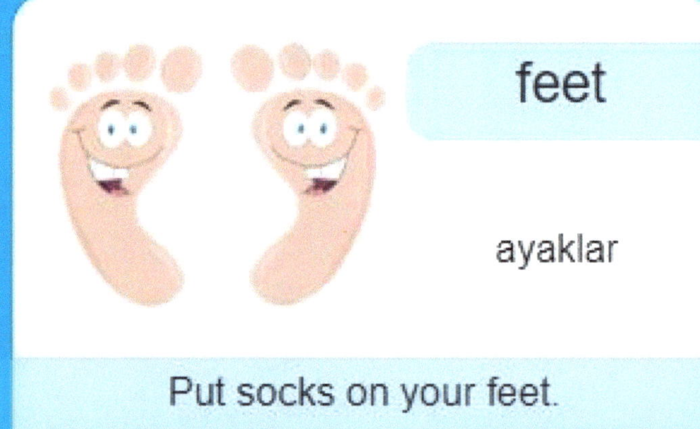

feet

ayaklar

Put socks on your feet.

few

az

She wanted a few more minutes.

food

gıda

They made a lot of food.

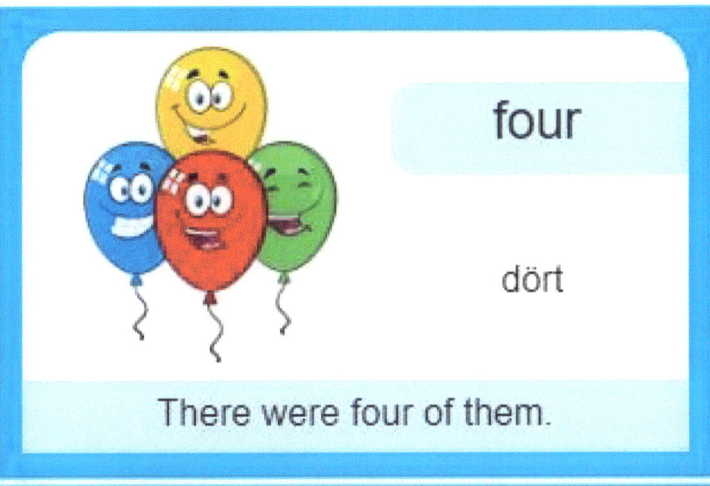

four

dört

There were four of them.

girl

kız

The girl wore pink shoes.

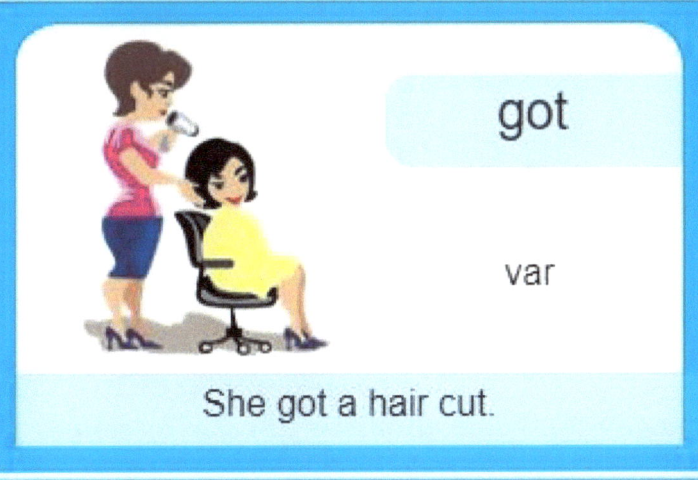

got

var

She got a hair cut.

group

grup

They were working in a group.

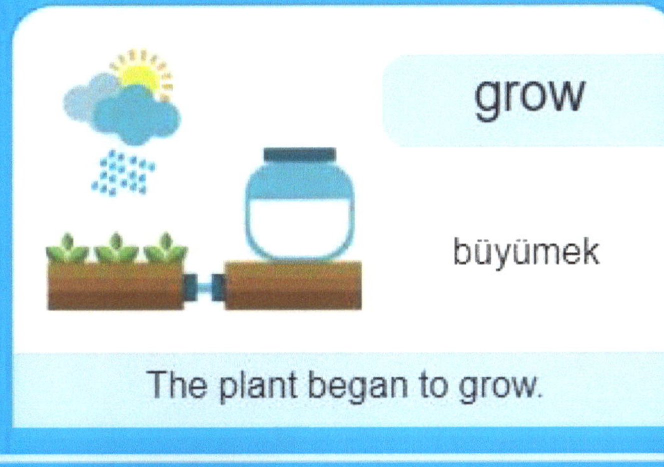

grow

büyümek

The plant began to grow.

hard

zor

He wore a hard hat.

head

kafa

He wore a cap on his head.

hear

duymak

You hear through your ears.

high

yüksek

She wore high heels.

idea

fikir

I have an idea!

important

önemli

It's important!

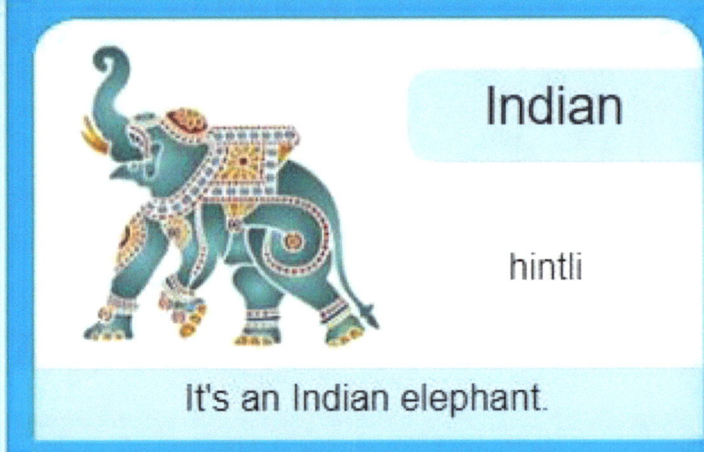

Indian

hintli

It's an Indian elephant.

it's

dır-dir

It's a tiger cub.

keep

tut

Can you keep a secret?

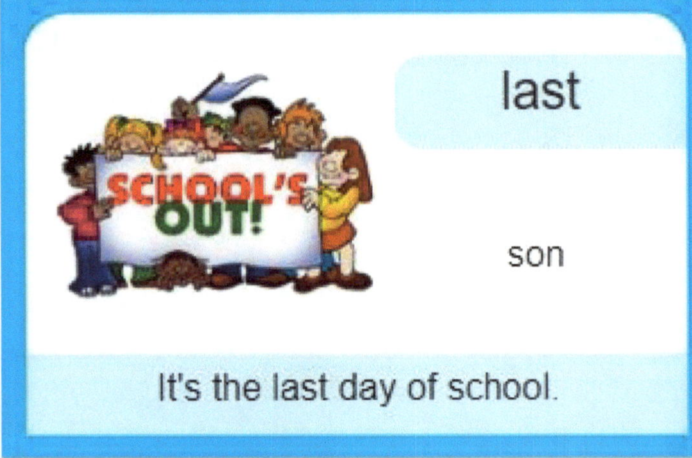

last

son

It's the last day of school.

late

geç

You're late.

leave

ayrılmak

He packed to leave.

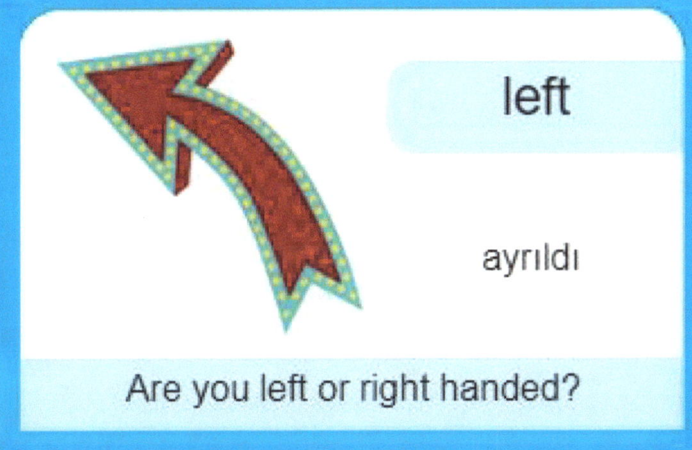

left

ayrıldı

Are you left or right handed?

let

izin vermek

Will you let me go fishing?

life

hayat

Life is about friends and family.

light

ışık

The light turned yellow.

list

liste

Here's my to-do list

might

belki

It might rain today.

mile

mil

It's a mile from here.

miss

özlemek

You may correct any you miss.

mountains

dağ

There are alot of mountains here.

near

yakın

We are near the beach.

never

asla

I've never broken my leg.

next

sonraki

Take the next step.

night

gece

You can see the stars at night.

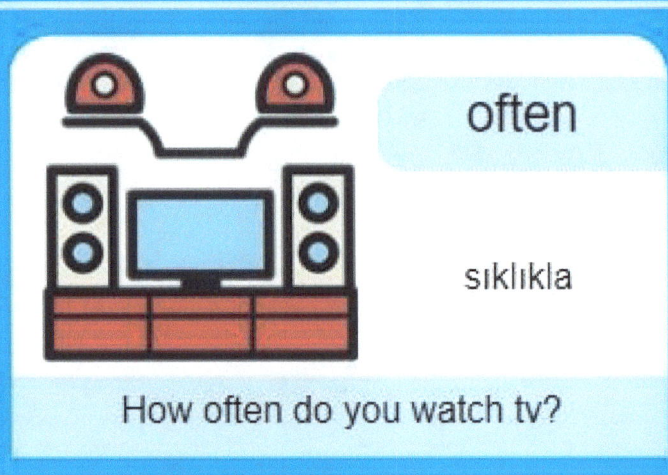

often

sıklıkla

How often do you watch tv?

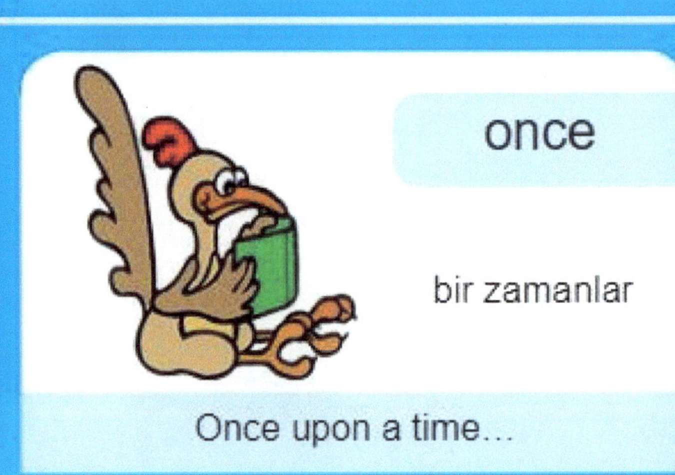

once

bir zamanlar

Once upon a time…

open

açık

The door is open.

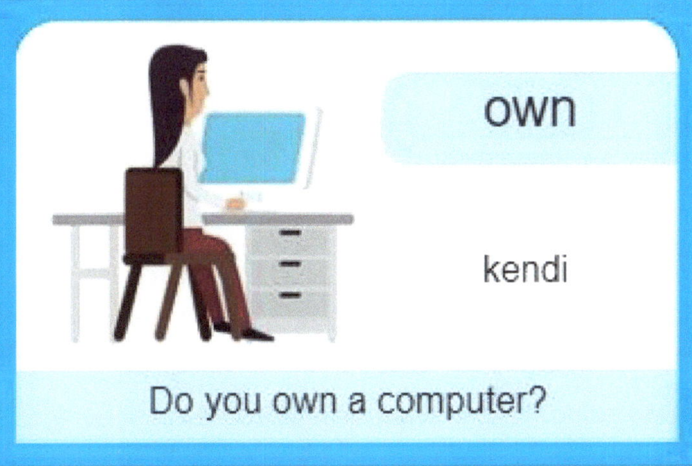

own

kendi

Do you own a computer?

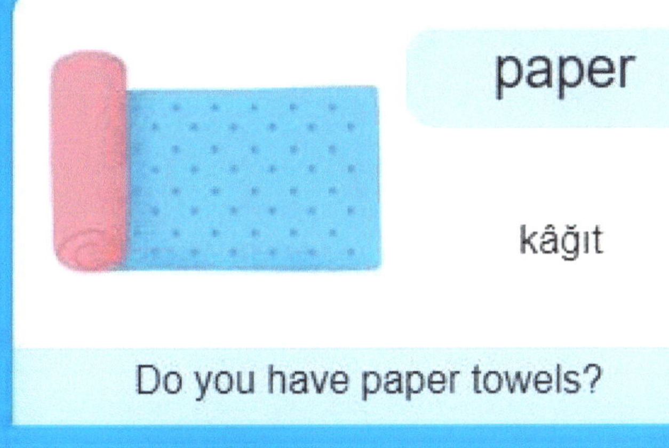

paper

kâğıt

Do you have paper towels?

plant

bitki

I will water the plant.

real

gerçek

Her real name is Sally.

river

nehir

The river is high.

run

çalıştırmak

He likes to run with his dog.

saw

görmek

We saw a UFO.

school

okul

Do you like school?

sea

deniz

The ship is at sea.

second

ikinci

She won second place.

seem

görünmek

You seem busy.

side

yan

Each side of a square is the same.

something

bir şey

Did you hear something?

sometimes

ara sıra

Sometimes we watch tv.

song

şarkı

We will sing a song.

soon

yakında

Dinner will be ready soon.

start

başlat

Start writing.

state

durum

Which state do you live in?

stop

dur

Do you see the stop sign?

story

hikaye

What's the story about?

talk

konuşma

Let's talk.

those

şunlar

Those are great cookies!

thought

düşünce

I thought the novel was good.

together

birlikte

They went shopping together.

took

almak

He took the last piece.

tree

ağaç

Did you decorate the tree?

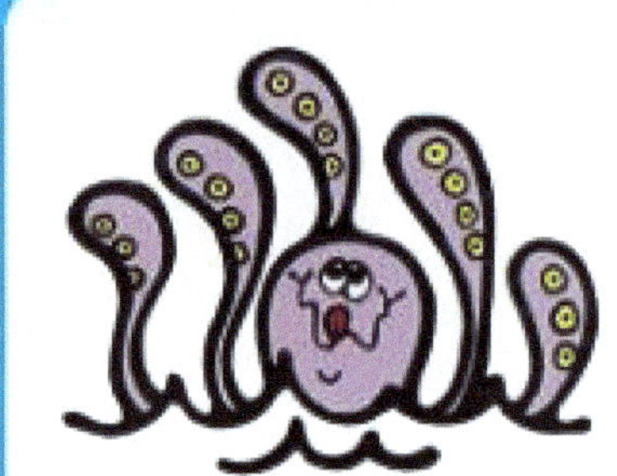

under

altında

It lives under the sea.

until

a kadar

I work until 5 o'clock.

walk

yürümek

We went for a walk.

watch

kol saati

Do you wear a watch?

while

süre

We had fun while skiing.

white

beyaz

They drew on the white board.

without

olmadan

I can't go without my backpack.

young

genç

Her kids are young.

across

karşısında

It's across the street.

against

karşısında

It's against the rules.

area

alan

There are no wild animals in this area.

become

olmak

It will become a butterfly.

best

en iyi

Do your best!

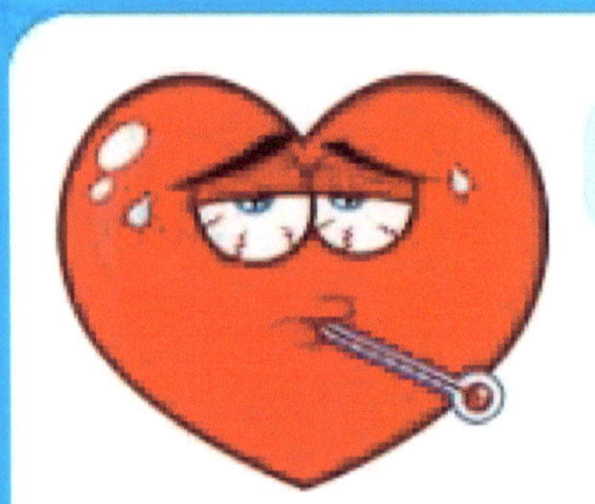

better

daha iyi

Feel better soon!

birds

kuş

There's a lot of birds.

black

siyah

He has a black cat.

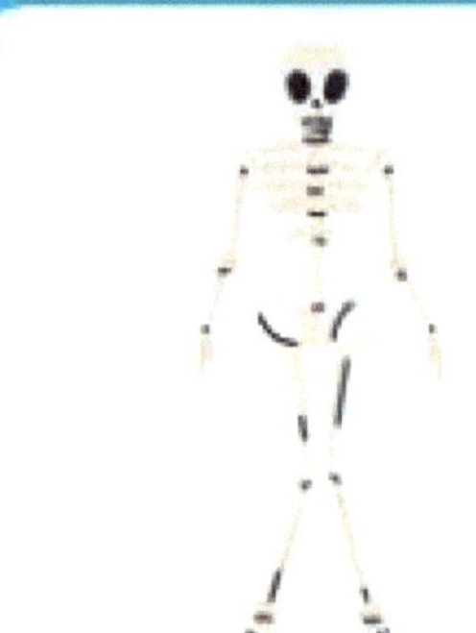

body

vücut

The body has a lot of bones.

certain

belirli

Certain words are harder than others.

cold

soğuk

It's cold outside.

color

renk

What is your favorite color?

complete

tamamlayınız

Did you complete your workout?